The Sound Of Silence

The Sound Of Silence

A BOOK OF OPERA POETRY

Austin Okorie

authorHOUSE®

AuthorHouse™
1663 Liberty Drive
Bloomington, IN 47403
www.authorhouse.com
Phone: 1-800-839-8640

Published by AuthorHouse   11/10/2012

ISBN: 978-1-4678-9034-2 (sc)
ISBN: 978-1-4678-9035-9 (e)

Contents

The Sound Of Silence 1

My Best Friend 5

Chidimma By Me 8

Sunrise At Dawn 12

Constantly 14

Ever Learning 16

To The One That
Used To Love Me 18

Good Journey 22

The Day We Parted 27

Going Back To Arizona 32

Waiting For Your Call 33

A Hopeful Mid-Day 37

Because I Belong To You 40

I Will Be Leaving You
Tomorrow 43

Friends Of Yesteryears 46

The Moon Is Shinning
Without You 49

You Are Right That
I Am Wrong 52

Angel In Confinement 56

The Battle Within 60

Book Keeping 63

A Pathetic Sunset 67

Responsibility 68

Nothing More To Lose 85

The Colour Of Love 88

The Dilemma Of A Seer 92

I Saw A Tombstone 100

Will You Marry Me 105

Rhythm Nature 107

The Last Straw 110

To The Unknown Soldier ... 112

Letters Of Gold—Tribute
To The Goloden Girl ... 113

In The Beginning 121

THIS BOOK IS DEDICATED TO MY

August-blessing

Ngozi A Okorie

My wife and best friend

AUTHORS NOTE

The touch of nature; the natural instinct, disposition or sensitivity to nature and natural operations. These have been an ever present attribute so obvious in my person.

The mountains, the hills, the quietness of the woods, The tranquility and enchantment of the so-called wild woods, have been a source of ecstatic revelry to me.

"The sound of silence" as the title for this work is a direct expression of my deep interaction and communion with nature.
Nature in its use here of course, refers to these natural elements, the sun, the moon, the trees,and grasses,the mountains and the hills,the rivers and the oceans.

Man, the head of all creation and the most rebellious, sounds a discordant note in the symphony of God's 'Organic composition,' hence

"*An awful bankruptcy is so obvious*
        with us
which by deliberate blindness
        we zealously enforce"
And
"*How much troubles*
        With us contemporal
Because we've ceased
        To be natural"

AUTHOURS NOTE

There is rhythm in nature,there is order as well.
If we remain natural we save ourselves
So much trouble

In intimate relationships,which form a major
Part of these work,these natural sensitivity is
Carried along to express my feelings,which
were mostly informed and inspired by real life
experiences; some good, some bad.
At times the most painful ones provided the
Most intense inspirations, as in "Nothing more
To lose," "The last straw" and others.

"I will therefore lift my eyes to the hills"

Yes I did; oftentimes and severally.
My help did come from the maker of the heavens
And the hills.

And all praise goes to him who endowed me
With the natural disposition that conceived this book.

The final word of this book is
A paradoxical epilogue—*"In the beginning"*
Naturally and necessarily, it is the final word.

AUSTIN OKORIE

ACKNOWLEDGEMENT

Many contributed to the making of this book
Some directly,others indirectly. Some made
Their contributions unknowingly. These simple
Words of appreciation is for all of you

Special thanks to my parents Innocent and Rebecca
Okorie, who provided us with a library before we
Were born. Thanks for the good foundation and the
Nurture you provided
To my wife, I cannot find the right words to
Express my gratitude, she is my best friend, my
Patience and my beauty, my noble one and faithful
And my most companionable companion.

> *"I am ever learning how*
> *Best to love you more*
> *And new ways*
> *to tell you so"*

Thanks to Dr Rosemary Obudulu. Thanks
Arc Godwin Chuks Okoye, for your immense
Brotherly care. Thanks to Eleanor Nwaba, wherever you
are,
I am very grateful to you. Thanks to Amarachi Laura
Onwutuebe, who typed and re-typed the manusripts.

To the sun and moon and the trees—my companions in
Solitude, my praise goes to the creator, who made them
And guided them with celestial discernment; to him that
Dwelleth in unapproachable light, for lightening up my
Mind.

AUSTIN OKORIE

The Sound Of Silence

On a large expanse
of winding land
Stand these heaps
of endless sand
Still they stood
with peaceful countenance
And non-could understand
their muted utterance.

The Sound Oe Silence

Then I came upon long stretches of
low green grass
As through the places of nature
I wandered in trespass

They swerved and swayed
in discordant unity
And none dared belittle
their common identity

They sang a song
with the voice of nature
I heard them sing
with joy and rapture

As they began to talk
and make their claim
I thought I heard them
Call all my name

The Sound Of Silence

They pledged to me
a great reward
That of my findings
not to say a word

Then I beheld the sky
so bright and blue
With yellow linings
not just a few

The grey that did
announce the rain
The gentle wind
that led their train

The heavens with Beauteous
cloud Configuration
Displayed with
Celestial discrimination

The Sound Of Silence

Then I looked
among the sons of men
If any a natural
man yet remain

Who could the
sound of silence but hear
The language of nature
so still and clear

But an awful bankruptcy is so
obvious with us
Which by deliberate blindness
we zealously enforce
Searching horizons
and the stars for insight
Ignoring these landmarks
that mitigates our plight.

My Best Friend

Can I hold your
hand my dear
And take you to
the mountains of the deer
To long grasslands
and the woods
Away from homes and
the neighborhoods
Give me that
hand of yours
That has been
so good to all of us
That has ministered
so much to my needs
Not counting my
shortcomings or misdeeds

My Best Friend

Let us go to the
quiet places of nature
Where the wild goats
do come for pasture
Let the gentle wind
play around your long hair
Covering your face so
beautiful and so fair
Swaying your long
skirt in sweet fascination
Exciting my fancy
and mild admiration
Words are unnecessary
at this time
For a thousand words
and one sublime

My Best Friend

Cannot tell me more
than this moment
Nor make so clear
this our testament
That it was a
leading from above
And how much
my life did improve
And my woes came
to an end
The day I called
you my best friend

Chidimma By Me

She speaks with courtesy
and quiet confidence
Of her unique nature,
this is but one evidence
Her beautiful eyes
so cool and bright
At once reveal her love
For what is good
The light of innocence,
her infectious humility
The essence of her
strength and ability

Chidimma By Me

These elements of
virtuous womanhood
Perpetually inspire
a cheerful attitude
She is not a perfect
personality perhaps
Nor is she immuned
from mistakes or mishaps
In friendship, none
could rival her faithfulness
Her loyalty and
undaunted hopefulness
In strife, she
smarts not to explain
Neither does resentment
induce her to complain

Chidimma By Me

She faces every duty
with graceful gentility
Motivated by none
but her sense of responsibility
Most companionable
companion I know
Non—discriminating
to the high and the low
I have one wish or
two I dare
To share with her each
week a day

Chidimma By Me

You will not miss her radiance
or fair dispose
The beauty and serenity
of her quiet repose
Her naturalness
and godly charisma
And lest I forget,
her name is "CHIDIMMA"

Sunrise At Dawn

On the horizon beautiful
colours appear
Yellowish pinks bidding
darkness disappear
Forerunners that tell us
the sun is awake
And its laborious journey
is about to make
The day is too young
to bare its mind
Quietness in the air, not
a stir from the wind
This early light of day
so gentle and cool
Will soon give way
to heat when the day is full

Sunrise At Dawn

This colours on the
horizon so multiplied
By invisible hands
bountifully supplied
Will soon lose their
individuality and hue
Their colours transform
to an all-white or blue
If I were the decider
of nature's acts unknown
I will overthrow some
eternal laws we've known
And establish the morning
light all day long
That all may live as
when we were young

Constantly

Let us go away
from here
The moon herself
can't forebear
She seems against
us so unfairly
And hastens to her rest
Quite so early
The moon herself
is jealous
Like everyone else
round about us
Let us go away
hence my dear
From every other company
close and near
The fulfillment we seek;
the peace and rest
Is best realized, away
from the rest

Constantly

See how your eye
out dazzles the moonlight
Your voice like the
singing bird of the night
Then tell me those
things gently
Which, yesterday you told
me intently
If you wish, say it in
other ways
That constantly, you
love me always
It will so much make
my day
That you said it again
today.

Ever Learning

I never changed on
my promise to you
Of everlasting love
and friendship true
Except that fact always
to mention
In all my ways;
words and action
Between my days
at school and now
When I knew little of
anything as thou
I cannot say I changed
so much
Not from our common
goal as such

Ever Learning

True, I learnt a lot to
be a builder
The organic principles
of nature to ponder.
To build house as
nature does
Humane and homely
houses for all of us
But perpetually
I remain a student of love
Restless adventurous life
As a dove
With my head
ever learning
And my heart
always discerning
How best to love
you more
And new ways to tell
you so.

To The One That Used To Love Me

Tell her 1 do not miss
her presence
For that indeed will not
make any sense

Strangely at times
I miss her face
Her unwomanliness and
lack of grace

Her artificiality and
pride of education
All she did in the
name of sophistication.

Tell her I am very happy
and still alive
Since she left me alone
a month and five

She opened for another
the door to my heart
And much peace to me
she did impart

To The One That Used To Love Me

One just as beautiful
or better of stature
And oh so lovely and
natural to my nature
Tell her more that I
wish her well
But never her absence
do I bewail?
That I'd like to offer
a helping hand
To make for her feet
a steadfast stand
Were I a dictator I
could that arrange
As nothing less
could make her change

<u>To The One That Used To Love Me</u>

Tell her she's actually the
one that is wrong
She rebuffed my gift and
despised my song
For lack of grace and
natural simplicity
Adorable attributes of
womanly integrity
Tell her I have need
to meet her again
I wish from her some
teachings to gain

To help fulfill the book
I make
I sure will pay
if she will take

To The One That Used To Love Me

To make a record
that men will learn
Plus the stipend
that she will earn

The story of a lady
so crude and rude
Sad imageries of a
perverted womanhood

Good Journey

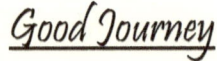

Fare thee well on your
journey
This our state is
neither fair nor funny

I know I will miss
you much
Your kind words and
gentle touch

Everything looks dull and
colourless
My heart so faint
and powerless

I know it well I will miss
you soon
But not so soon as
before noon

Good Journey

My days are full of
longing
My night an endless
mourning

The hours are too
far between
As with my woes I battle
to win
Good journey dear, love,
good journey
This our state is neither
fair nor funny

This month will be the
longest in the year
Though it's a February,
let's forebear

Good Journey

Let us then accept
this present truth
And get to our problem
and its root.

To live without each other
but for now
But all the temptings around
us disallow

For sadness of heart
and the lack of glow
And all the tears they
urge to flow

These and all else that
plague the heart
Help us in life to define
our part

Good Journey

If only we learn to out-live
our sorrow
And brighten our hearts with
promises of tomorrow

Good journey dear love
good journey
This our state is neither
fair nor funny

As you go on your journey
and as you come
With love and smiles
to warm our home

Good Journey

To share with me your
joy anew
The kind that is known
to just a few

A joy that will bid our
grief disappear
A joy far greater than
the sorrows we bear.

The Day We Parted

It was a day of
mist and cloud
My sorrows urge me to
cry aloud
The day was neither bright
nor dark
The birds could not sing
nor the dogs bark
Everything was to me
black or blank
I lost appetites for food
to be frank

The Day We Parted

The flowers lost their colours
their significance and sweet odours
The grasses lost their green
the river by the woods a picture less screen
The sky lost its colours
blue and bright
Assuming a countenance
sad as the night
This day hath done my heart

so much harm
All beauty to my eyes
lost their charm.

The Day We Parted

Pathetically, we said
reluctant "goodbyes"
With heaviness of heart
and tears in her eyes

The 'wicked' taxi bore
her away
Leaving me with none but
my sorrows to stay

Increasing in giant strides
the distance between us
I wished I had by me
our faithful horse.

The Day We Parted

I turned homewards and
about to go
Thinking of the lonely days
i must soon undergo

And was confronted by the
lonely mountains far
From which my affection
I did transfer

My previous companions
in solitude
Which despised me now with
unfriendly attitude

And denied me any
helps from above
As they mocked me for
falling in love!

Going Back To Arizona

To the plains and desert
places
Where there are none
or few faces

To the place devoid of
men's perversions
To behold more of God
and his creations

When I turned my back
on you
Melancholy overwhelmed
me like the dew

From your shores indeed
I did depart
But I left behind with
you my heart

Going Back To Arizona

To Arizona yet I am
going back
Where I am full and know
no lack

By the beauties around
and their enchantments
That move my heart by
quiet statements
Come with me my faithful
company
Let's sing to us our
joyful litany

Telling tales on those
arizona brooks
Look for me in its most
enchanted nooks

Waiting For Your Call

Waiting for you, waiting for
your call
You did assure me if
you recall

That this day of all will
be my day
That you'll lend your
time to me and stay

I am full of longing and
without respite
Though the day is come,
but that inspite

I watch relentlessly the sluggish
arm of the clock
My oak paneled door, its
handle and lock

<u>*Waiting For Your Call*</u>

Do you remember me as
you do before
Or you leap with the years once
out of every four

Upon my bed I fight a
lost battle
As my loaded brain
sleep do rattle

A heavy doze hangs
upon my eye lid
A great favour indeed at
this hour of need

But I'll rather be hurt
cry and weep
Than meet you face-to-face
in my sleep

A Hopeful Mid-Day

It all began last night
I saw you in my dream
Benevolent assurances from
the spirit realm

Somehow I could not
make it today to church
I was not downcast or
indisposed as such

But I confess candidly this
day of the Lord
That I was swept
off-course, as if by a flood

And I found myself hearded
for this familiar field
Calmness on my mind and
with joyousness filled
i sat down to write and my
heart felt so free
It's so homely here under
the shade of this tree

A Hopeful Mid-Day

From the distance i hear
voices of intercession
Contending earnestly
the yokes of oppression

Maybe you are somewhere
now praying for my cause
That heaven lay for my
feet a smoother course

A Hopeful Mid-Day

The Angels have noted
your petitions this day
Granting the blessing of
this August mid-day

Deliverance has come for
my hurt and my ills
Like the calmness on
the face of the hills

<u>Because I Belong To You</u>

To be too lowly, to be too noble
Not in any wise to be ignoble

When I gave my heart
to you
I gave to you my
body too

That in menial things
and common
Not just at your bid
or summon

Because I Belong To You

My allegiance stedfast
will show
In single mindedness my
devotion bestow

For you my dear
nothing is too good
As no circumstance
distracts your happy mood

Nor anything beneath my
dignity to undertake
Once our love and
loyalty, is at stake

<u>Because I Belong To You</u>

I will surely do it with
more and more zeal
My faithfulness and
trust thus reveal

If it will tell the world
better
That I belong to you
now and later

<u>I Will Be Leaving You</u>
<u>Tomorrow</u>

This day is going
so fast,
For the midnight hour
already is past
Who will this sorrow
mostly bear
As to our hearts this
sharing we endear
But I will be leaving
you tomorrow
With all the tears and
sighs that will follow
I will be leaving you
tomorrow
And you will need a
helping hand to borrow

I Will Be Leaving You Tomorrow

Let's pretend I am gone
already
For the lonesome hours to
come let's be ready
Let's bear the pains of
tomorrow in us today
And feel the better when
at last we meet the day
I wish i could help you
dearest friend
Forestal this sad and
unfortunate trend
For as helpless as you
so I am
I mean not to deny you
my supporting arm

I Will Be Leaving You
Tomorrow

But our sharing endures till
the morning light
When our sorrows
loom in our sight
I will be leaving you
Tomorrow
Be strong my dear and
beat this sorrow
I'll leave a piece of my
voice so comforting
To take you through
these nights of longing

Friends Of Yesteryears

(Dialogue with a dried tree trunk)

Have the years seduced
your former affections
You showered by many
intimate confessions
Turning yesterdays truths
to a lie
I cannot on your
faithfulness again rely
Pray, take off that
expressionless face
And let your feelings
come to surface

Friends Of Yesteryears

Remember the past
how we used to play
And remove this
countenance you now display
All my life 1 hate to
Pretend
To deceive by did
that which I intend
That a few years
out of touch
Has changed your mind
by so much
Spare me a little smile
or more
Or let the tears flow
as before

Friends Of Yesteryears

I am familiar with
either of the two
Pleased by your rejoicing
and sadness too
The deep impressions on
our hearts stand
Were written not
on tables of sand
For they withstood
the flood and the rain
By the river, were not
washed down the drain
If you recall your
Yesteryears remarks
Should I believe the
Waves have washed their marks?

The Moon Is Shinning Without You

Ten days ago, you left
our home
And far from me you
went to Rome
To the call of duty, the
job you hold
1 can't say exactly if its
warm or cold
But over our neighbourhood
the moon is out
With the night and darkness
to do a bout
But her glorious beam
does not my heart fill
Nor remove this lonesomeness
which I feel

The Moon Is Shinning
Without You

Shadows around me yet
prevails
Portraits of all
my state entails
Go tell the moon now
to wait
For she is ten days
just too late.
For my heart and thine
are one
From the day my love
you won
And you're gone away
with hoth
I dare declare it
with an oath.

The Moon Is Shinning Without You

Now that you are so
far away
No words can describe
the sad affair
For though the moon is
all out and bright
I see more of darkness
and the night
The essence of her beauty
is gone apart
The language of her brightness
that touch my heart.

<u>You Are Right
That I Am Wrong</u>

My unreasoning self
took hold of me
I knew the way,
but failed to see
And how nearly I had
gone astray
Without your courage to
point the way
You are right that
I am wrong
I knew it well, you are
faithful and strong

You Are Right
That I Am Wrong

To stand alone and
declare the fact
When the truth is
against our act
Did I hear you saying?
that you are sorry?
But I tell you indeed, you
are not to worry.

You Are Right That I Am Wrong

For I am the one to
bear the blame
As you denied yourself
to save our name
Don't regret you stood
for the truth
It's not in vain
that your name is Ruth
You are quite right that
1 am wrong
I'll get right within
before its long.

Angel In Confinement

So full of life yet gentle
in appearance
Dear little Angel girded
with forebearance
My prayer for you
earnestly offered
Is that you reach your
destination unconquered
Not by sacrificing the
honour you nurture
Nor mortgaging the glory
you own by nature.

Angel In Confinement

I wish I could help you
dear Angel
But I refrain to covet
a celestial evangel

I am not even sure you
need a helping hand
From your sweet countenance
and the colourful band

Secured firmly round
your seemless gown
Your face that defies even
a momentary frown

Angel In Confinement

Good journey gentle
messenger from above
As you course through your
path like a dove
I'm glad you have access
to the throne of grace
Away from this generation
of ungodly race
Your confinement forbids
my ponder
To witness closely your
beauty and its wonder

Angel In Confinement

I watch from here your
advance with your fellow
Bidding you God—speed
with the one you follow
I know your portion shall
be honour and favour
For your endurance,
patience and godly labour
Every place you go
shall be beauty and light
Spare me your radiance till
you're out of my sight

The Battle Within

In all thy gettings
get thou knowledge
This the Holy Book saith
to all that may care
I have seen in this life
a strange contradiction
For he that eats most
do hunger the more
As I went out to fill myself
with life's delicacies
In this liberty, no restraints
to observe

The Battle Within

I came back less of all
I wished to be
Then I took my liberty
away and far
To face the battle within
and to win
I lost my comfort
for a season or so
In my flesh and bones
I felt the pains
The pains of restraint
and denial of self

The Battle Within

I began to see more
into ordinary things
To excuse the sun for
moving so slowly
That a child should
walk well before he runs
I began to see why the day
is longer
When viewed from an
empty stomach
But the night prevents the evening
on a day of merriment

The Battle Within

Excellence in all my doings
I now desired
As I learnt to give more time
doing ordinary things
I began to grow into
the man I loved
Seeing that you begin to live
after you have died to self
I fought this grim battle
within and won
Kept alive by how much
I had learnt to forego!

Book Keeping

(Tribute to Eudorah—The libra princess)
Of those that love you,
when you compose a list
Put my name foremost
there in their midst
I confess sincerely that I lost
in the game
Though not utterly disappointed
in my claim
It may not be your fault
nor am I to blame
That after so long
we fall behind our aim
I tell you frankly that
you've won
And 1 have lost in all
areas but one

Book Keeping

My only victory being that
i lost to your person
In the event of it all,
I learnt a lesson
That heaven directs
the affairs of mankind
If we submit to the gentle
urgings of the mind.
1 cannot forget those
sacrifices sincerely made
When our hearts
by lovely passions were fed
How you traversed land and sea
to say you cared
And I traveled the states
to see how you fared
If anything but truth
inspired your deed
I was completely
unaware of the need

Book Keeping

When you make your
book of remembrance
Let your heart move by
quiet temperance
Resist the language of
the critic
As to why our lives
failed to stick
From all these realities
we see
You should have motivated
the best in me.

A Pathetic Sunset

As you walk by my side to this
end of the road
So rough and so narrow with
few places broad
We walked on with joy
playfulness and smiles
Now I go back alone
just counting the miles
Now I will turn back
and leave you alone
So be on your way
and be on your own
I shall not go beyond this
wood plank
That bridges this familiar
river bank

A Pathetic Sunset

I only wish to make the
journey short
To save our hearts from
a more damaging hurt
1 never knew today will
mark our last goodmorn
With many unspent days
now to mourn
Should I surrender you to
this circumstantial trend
That had denied me
many a familiar friend
Bidding you farewell as
you depart
Though it's the farthest
thing from my heart

A Pathetic Sunset

The shadows on the
river lengthens
The strength of the
sunshine weakens
This glorious evening sun
Only excites a pathetic song
I will not go beyond
this place
Of precious moments
shared with grace
Do not mistake my
resolution firm
As despising
to our lifelong aim

A Pathetic Sunset

I thought 1 have seen
all heartaches my due
And recalling my sorrows
counted them few
But to part with you at
such friendly hour
Of sunset, cloud play and
this present lilly flower
Is too painful a price
to pay
Saddest a moment, another
goodbye to say

Responsibility

Tribute to my Noble One.

It's not that you ceased
to thrill my heart as before
Nor that your charm
diminished in any way
My unwillingness to stay
is against my own will
I really want to be with you
To spend many a moment
of unuttered communication
As we've often done in the past

Responsiblity

Tribute to my Noble One

But my head revolted
against this
And took the lead
over my heart
The man in me stood up
to the challenge of integrity
For its time to face the
responsibility
which I owe a responsible woman
To undo the burdens
overtasking the usefulness
of a utility wife

<u>Responsibility</u>

Tribute to my Noble One

I cannot fully express my gratitude to you
No; not for the commitment
you've shown
Nor for the one I see in your eyes
But it's no surprise to me
For you are only being
true to your colour
For before you said "I do"
you knew the many
mistakes of my youth
And a few shortcomings afterwards
did not challenge your faithfulness.
I will go away this month,
and the next, and the following one.
And if it takes more time than I propose
I know you will wait for me.

Responsibility

Tribute to my Noble One

For I go to explore my fortune
and fight the battle of fate
a common destiny for all manhood.
But I am all too eager
to return back to you
When I shall be ready to take up
the duties ordained for a husband.

Responsibility

Tribute to my Noble One

If the head of every woman is the man
The heart of every man.
will be the woman.
Then I shall be ready to offer
the support and direction
Which the heart requires from the head.
And I will have nothing against myself
When you spread those familiar arms again.
To welcome the one you've
chosen to love and to cherish.
Till death do us part, if at all it can!

Nothing More To Lose

(Lamentations to Eleanor)

A loss is painful to
the heart
By a full measure
or in part
A loss leaves the loser less
If he loses not everything else
Depending on the nature
of loss
Yes! Its origin and
source.
It brings despair and
Confusion
Estrangement and lonely
depression

Nothing More To Lose

Through my life not
far spent
A few lessons in loss
have learnt
I have lost my time
and throne
To some extent my state
has shown
But the greatest loss
steers my way
And helpless I stand
watching in despair
As my most cherished possession
passes by me
The legal possession of
another to be

Nothing More To Lose

—Lamentation to Eleanor—

I may soon loose
Again
This time with great sorrow
and pain
A loss that will my
person unsettle
And the better part of
me belittle
A loss that will my
tears recall
Shed for my past
failures and all
Oh! That this cup will pass
by me
With its painful consequences
which I see

Nothing More To Lose

The thought of it has
left me cold
The grim shadow of an
event foretold
Can I bear the separation
The loneliness and desertion
How long can I live
with it
As my lonesome heart
doth sink beneath
Surely it will not be
very long
Before all that is right
is gone wrong
For a part of me with
it is lost
The better part of me
leaving the worst.

Nothing More To Lose

My little world is falling apart
Whose existence I saw in part
My little world of
contented quietness
Builded on love, truth
and faithfulness
Immaterial substances we
greatly esteemed
Born of this world but
from it redeemed.
Pretence and selfishness
we despised
Truth and graceful simplicity
so highly we priced
My little world with a
Beginning
Which was to have no
ending

Nothing More To Lose

It is coming to an
end
A purpose I never
did intend.
I believed so much in my
world of two
With its devotions and
faithfulness true
Patiently had I waited
on the line
When in its fullness I
shall have it for mine
But it may never
come true
Oh how painful to
I lose you.

Nothing More To Lose

The embodiment of
my affection and love
And the virtues of goodness
given us from above
I have nothing more
to lose
With no options now
to choose
As well 1 have nothing
more to gain
Having no heart to
love again.
My life without you
is unwholesome
A haunted life
of loneliness and boredom
I will be living on
my half-life
Which may not be
a long-life

Nothing More To Lose

But who cares for
Longevity
If it's only to live
under depravity.
Disappointments and
broken dreams
Emptiness and lifelessness
of waterless streams
Wasted love, that hurts
like a sword
Infinite chastisements
of an unfriendly rod
Nightmares that were in my
wounded heart now recalled
And the daily torment
of a lost world.

Nothing More To Lose

I long for a
Release
From this heart pain and
unease
Shall I then myself
resign
To this half-life
of woe unbenign
Or else myself
Deny
On the mask of pretense
rely
Shall I about the streets
Go
Wearing on my face
so
Artificial cheerfulness
and smile
Hypocrisy, vain deceptions
as a style
Things I learnt
to abhor from my youth
Vanity and all that
despise the truth

Nothing More To Lose

May be they have a
cause
Artificial men and pretenders of
course
May be they know
Better
And will make it known
later
That in a world
of so much wrong
All we need is a
heart that is strong
For truth, faithfulness
and sincerity
Receives a hurt with
severity

Nothing More To Lose

(Lamentations to Eleanor)

But strength of heart without these
Bears the hurt
with much ease.
Henceforth do I no longer blame a man
Who, for previous hurts adopts a plan
Through which his life to transform
From grass to grace to conform
Though his actions
make him strange
Yet do 1 excuse him and his change

Nothing More To Lose

On my own part I
will wait
With all my heartache and its weight
Across my darkening sky
A sylver-lining could yet fly
They could be deliverance
from above
Divine intervention, for the sake
of my love.
My little world could
yet abide
And there 1 and mine
in peace reside.
They tell me the future
will bring the best
But i desire no more
from love than my first

Nothing More To Lose

(Lamentations to Eleanor)

To her I owe much thanks
and gratitude
So wonderful and comely
of womanhood
1 will be my best and
wait in peace
And non of my professions
to truth dismiss.
Romeo from his Juliet
could not depart
Though friends and families
bid them apart
But my love than Romeo's
is stronger
It's desires and dedications
such a wonder
I will go therefore the
extra mile
If to my clouded face to bring
again a smile.

The Colour Of Love

On a mid-summer day I looked around
Much beauty and gladness did me surround
The sunshine and the
fun fair
The quiet evening and
the warm air
Our flower garden and
its fragrance
That brought feelings
of old remembrance.
I rejoiced with my companion
Fair
Wishing for no other
fellowship to share

The Colour Of Love

Until the going down of
the sun
I realised my companion
was gone
She is made for sunshine not the dark night
For good times and when all is right.
I had to face the dark night all alone
With its coldness and
intents unknown
I braced myself and made
to stay
Till this distant companion
came my way

The Colour Of Love

She offered her help
without reward
The much I did was
to say a word.
A word of thanks for the
price she paid
She did assure me she
is much repayed
All her wish was to share
my solitude
To lighten the darkness with
friendly attitude
1 began to see in this
darkest night
Brighter and brighter till
the morning light

<u>The Dilemma Of A Seer</u>

If there were more clues
as to the way of the eagle
Nor why the ocean
will not exceed its boundary
Then I could hope to express
this unutterable instinct
But I find myself in a blissful dilemma
Stretched to a limit by friendly forces
That urge me to say things
beyond my utterance

The Dilemma Of A Seer

But there are no words so articulate
Nor groanings so profound
to speak the refined
language of these feelings within
To the mountains
I sought for help
By their awesome size
and majestic countenance
The silhouette of their smooth
outline
against the background of a
retiring evening sun
But they inspire me with more thought
And enhance my
Bewilderment

The Dilemma Of A Seer

The trees and the grasses
my friends of long standing
Showed a willingness to assist
To their domain I did resort
And many a faithful
evening there I shared
Observing when an inch
was added to their height
But how can I express
this enchantment
To this generation of wanton
and baseless busy men
But my gratitude to providence

The Dilemma Of A Seer

That I am not past the age of growth
I shall go to bed tonight
To wake up tomorrow
If I have the good fortune
I shall do the same the day after
Until I have grown beyond
the age of my problem
Then I shall speak
with exuberance
The great truths of life
Beyond the eyes;
within the soul
Then I shall be freed
from this dilemma
The dilemma of a seer,
a prophet and a poet.

I Saw A Tombstone

Once upon a long
journey bent
As thro this wild
wood I went
I came upon a ground
so spacious
And knew at once
it's to someone quite precious
I wondered about
in a low tone
And turning around
I saw a tombstone

I Saw A Tombstone

And a figure that
moved out of the wood
The only living soul
within the neighborhood
He could not be more
than thirty years
Judging as it were by
the frame he bears
The lines upon his face I fain
Is not the work of age but pain
He called to me with
the voice of a sage
I knew I misjudged the
years of his age
Way fairer, what beholdest
thou,? he said
Art thou an adversary?
or art thou come to my aid

I Saw A Tombstone

Why do you gaze so long?
on an epitaph?
Be on your way and let
me mourn on your behalf.
For I am a man of
endless sorrow
That ends only when
my death must follow
Said I, I'm on a long
journey bent
And through this wide
wood I am sent
Why art thou of such
a sorrowful mood?
Tell me thy cause, for
worse or for good.
Way fairer he said,
Thou art too questful
And askest thou
Why I am sorrowful?

I Saw A Tombstone

Well, I am a youth as thou
of a beautiful dream
My life with joy was
full to the brim
Two and ten years ago
with the love of my Youth
We came to this wood in
innocency and truth
According to tradition which
for long we hold
To share the evenings
and the setting sun behold
To welcome the coming night
in each others company
And with same parting memories
endure the night's tyranny.

I Saw A Tombstone

So we came on that fateful day
About she went to
sing and to play
Then she saw a flower
on that spot stand
It was pink in colour,
a most beautiful brand.
She stretched herself
to pick the stem
To pluck the flower
and to hold it firm
But that was the end
of the plans we made
That very moment
was our farewell bade

I Saw A Tombstone

On her hand a serpent
fastened its fangs
She cried and tried but on it hangs
I rushed to her
but my aid was late
I could not think nor
contemplate
She cried and swooned
with her last effort
The agony of death's
cruel discomfort
She died in my arms
shortly afterwards
As I lifted my tearful
eyes heavenwards

I Saw A Tombstone

I cannot forget the pains of her death
Nor my promise before
her very last breath
I was twenty years
by then I remember
I will be thirty-two by
middle of this September
Be on your way
way fairer, you look so pale
Lest I weary you with
my melancholy tale.
In faithfulness to my love
I am here
And will be here till
my death, I fear

<u>I Saw A Tombstone</u>

Be on your way the day
is far spent
Pursue the adventure on
which you are bent
On your way back you
may find I am gone
And there you will see
another tombstone
An epitaph that tells
of my life and death
And you are my witness
as I go from the earth.

Will You Marry Me

I believe in love, I believe in marriage
Noblest institution of our ancient heritage
That it is a good thing
to find a wife
Amiable companion in the
journey of life
So will you marry me I say
To share my life for all
1 care
For I have seen in your friendship
For my life, a right partnership

Will You Marry Me

That you do my feelings understand
And my shortcomings withstand
My deep feelings quite unspoken
And utterances half
with-holden
Those solemn eyes of yours
With the light of trust so obvious
Assures my heart to stay at rest
To shun every trial, to
dare every test.

Will You Marry Me

Then will you marry me
my dearly
I promise to share my
life sincerely
In singleness of heart
with you alone
Devote my life to
enhance your own
I do not promise you
everything money can buy
Neither do 1 refuse for
a season to say goodbye
But always will I your
opinion respect
And dispense to you, the
same, which I expect

<u>Will You Marry Me</u>

All within my heart I
do conspire
My tender love will
thus inspire
Will you marry me
my beloved
To share your life I
have resolved
Making each day fresh
and exciting
With the warmth and
hope of a sun rising
Our love each day thus growing
On the stepping stones of time ever flowing
Let us strive to out do
one another
In sacrificial goodness
each for the other

Will You Marry Me

It is always a more
excellent way
And from heaven attracts a bounteous repay
Darling will you marry
me today
To realize in truth the
dreams we share
Truly, I believe in love,
I believe in marriage
Noblest institution of our ancient heritage.

Rhythm Nature

Yesterday,fore runner of today
          Is gone
Today,its appointed course
          Half has done
Tommorrow will come,
          If we but live to see
To brighten the mountains
          The valleys and the sea
The spring, the summer,
          The winter and the fall
With their colds, bounties,
          Beauties and all
How in their appointed time
          They come and go
And their perculiar moods
          Patiently undergo

Rhythm Nature

One season taking
      Taking over from another
While we but watch
        And wonder
Not knowing the end
      Or beginning of any
Whether their days be
       Few or many
How constant and consistent in this
      Their eternal appointment
How all nature sings with abandonment
And how much troubles
      With us contemporal,
Because we've ceased to be natural

The Last Straw

Like the waves that chide
      The embanking shores
Threatening with overflow
      Their sandy floor
Now we must give up
      Each the other
With all the promises
      Made one another
This incompartibility so obvious
Declare plainly I cannot be yours
I have faulted you once too many
Of less devotion commitment and poor company

The Last Straw

You accused me of selfishness
           And emty professions
Untrue love and
           Lip-deep confessions
But let me once more
           Mention this truth
'That must bear in future
           A blessed fruit
You are the only one
           I cared about
Of all faces I've seen
           From north to south
Frankly, you ought to have
           Waited a while
For the day that will
           Bring your smile
For when a man hath
           Given his heart
It's a little thing
           To also give his hat

The Last Straw

My chiefest fault as you report
Is poor habit of material support
I deny not your need of materials seen
But the greater gifts indeed
        Are mostly unseen
I thought we can endure today
        And dare its sorrow
Since we expect for you
And me a brighter tomorrow.

To The Unknown Soldier

To many in the land
he's quite unknown
Yet there be a few
that may have known
Of these men few, 1
know but twain
The child and the
girl that bore the pain
To me unknown soldier
If thou be alive
Must give an answer
so long as I live.
Of the many offences
that you are charged
To plead your guilt
or be discharged
Why you left that
girl alone to shame
With the child that
should have borne your name

To The Unknown Soldier

Until this man from
God was sent
Who is "guiltless" by
nature an intent.
I do not hate you, nor
seek your ill
But I wish to know you
your mind and will
If you are humble and
of a godly fear
Heaven grant your
prayers a listening ear.
But if you are proud,
defamer and liar
Heaven be your
judge dear Unknown Soldier.

—Letters Of Gold—
Tribute To The Goloden Girl

Do you have a destiny with sorrow?
Is it chance or mischance,
That predispose you for continual tears?
I though that nature itself
Would have respected such generous beauty
As she bestowed on you
Or are you paying for such
Lavish endowments?
Why does the harmless often
Come to harm?
Why is friendliness not always
Rewarded with good companionship?
Why is a woman of honour crowned
With sorrow and loneliness
If character is the seed of destiny
Why does a good character beget
A destiny of sorrows

Letters Of Gold

Your beautiful name "Obioma",
So compatible with your comeliness,
Run at variance with the
Circumstances of your life
I had expected your friends to
Surround you with support and sympathy.
To declare your innocence
And your goodness.

Letters Of Gold

To tell the world the real person
You are
And if nobody does it
I will be the one to do it
For I still believe in you
I see beyond the scar
Upon your face
I see the garland of honour
Upon your "princess" outfit
I see a new destiny of hope
And happiness
A destiny of beauty
And blessedness
For the old destiny was consumed
By fire
The fire that threatened
Your very life

Letters Of Gold

But you were not consumed
Yes, your body was torched by fire
Leaving those "marks of honour"
The marks of a new beginning
The significance of a new destiny

The ingredients of life
Had composed within you
A heart of gold
The various indices of womanly honour,
attested to your favour
The enchantement of your eyes;
The light and language of your smiles,
Still defies my comprehension
They call you the golden girl
I contested that title
When I knew you not
Now I realize how far I was
From the truth
When I doubted your virtues

Letters Of Gold

No wonder the gods resented
Your continued stay on earth
And with fierce indignation
Plotted your demise
But your guardian
Angel Proved stronger than them
Your victory was not surprising though
Since you are also an angel

You will not cry again "golden girl"
For I will always be there for you
I will bear the light for you
By night
I will share your beautiful smiles by sunrise

Letters Of Gold

I will listen to the music
Of your voice
And revel in the beauty
Of your countenance
I will hold your hand
In my own
To keep you steady, to keep you calm
I will look into those beautiful eyes
Of yours
Where I always see love
Commitment and care
I will be unto you
A true friend
A trusted one
A faithful companion
A willing support
An everlasting love!
And when the chronicles are done
My name will be there
With yours
Written side by side
In letters of gold.

In The Beginning

(An Epilogue)

In the beginning, I really
did intend
To share with you this
truth at the end
You know how much to me you meant
The several truths from you I learnt
The love and good times
we've shared
Till this day how beautifully
we've fared
I will tell you this in the Last
To abide your heart
when all is past

In The Beginning

Of him who is the way,
truth and life
Whom we owe allegiance
as bride and a wife
Its true we love each other so dearly
Then let's consider this
truth more sincerely.
I hate to think of that inevitable day
When from two of us
one is taken away
As our affection cannot
stay the separation
Let's be up and commence a preparation

In The Beginning

He ever seeks admittance
into our being
His presence revealed in
all we are seeing
We have good evidence
to trust his promise
To honour and follow
without compromise
Partaking of his overwhelming
Sacrifice
As our efforts in this will not
suffice
I commend you to him that
liveth eternally
Who in time and beyond will
keep you perpetually
To him who is able to make you stand
When I am too weak
to hold your hand!